THE NIGHTLY WORD

31 Scriptures For Nightly Prayer
With Affirmations

LESLEY A

THE NIGHTLY WORD
31 SCRIPTURES FOR NIGHTLY PRAYER WITH AFFIRMATIONS
by LESLEY A

Printed in the United States of America.

ISBN 9781498496094

www.xulonpress.com

Jenelle & Jahnaya

Jenelle -
God is in charge

Jahnaya -
Jesus loves you

Lesley A

This prayer book is inspired by my grandson Aidan. He prays with me and for me whenever I'm staying with him at night while his mother is at work. Thank you, Aidan, for your prayers.

To my other two grandchildren, Anayah and Logan, I love you both.

Love,
Grandma

INTRODUCTION

The purpose of this devotional is to help readers maintain a habit of nightly prayer, and to inspire them in their walk with God through Scripture readings that are centered on experiencing God's presence, His protection, and His peace. Readers who are struggling through life's difficulties will be uplifted and encouraged to know that God is a God for all time. He is with us always, and He will never leave us nor forsake us. Psalm 91:11 says, "For He shall give His angels charge over you, to keep you in all your ways" (NKJV).

GRACE AND PEACE
Lesley A.

A NIGHTTIME POEM

Now I lay me down to sleep,
I pray the Lord my soul to keep.

Guide me safely through the night,
And wake me in the morning light.

If I should live another day,
I pray the Lord to guide my way.

When in the morning light I wake,
Show me the path of love to take.

CONTENTS

NIGHT 1 – PRESENCE OF GOD

Psalm 91:1 (NKJV)

"He who dwells in the secret place of the Most High shall abide under the shadow of the Almighty."

You live in God's presence, and He lives in yours, surrounding, enfolding, protecting, and shielding you from anything harmful. A feeling of joy and peace comes into your mind and heart as you rest within the presence of God's love. All fear and anxiety leaves you. Tension, strain, and feelings of aloneness are banished when you know that God guides you safely through every moment of the day and night. Whatever you do, wherever you may be, God is with you. Safe and secure in His love, you rest joyously and fearlessly in the path of peace, happiness, and security.

Affirmations:

I rest peacefully in the presence of God.

I am safe and secure in God's love.

I am never alone: God is always with me.

Prayer for Tonight:

Heavenly Father, I thank You for keeping me in Your divine presence. Take away any feelings of unrest in my being so that Your peaceful presence will surround me and my household.

NIGHT 2–**PROTECTION**

Isaiah 41:10 (NKJV)

> "Fear not, for I am with you. Be not dismayed, for I am your God. I will strengthen you. Yes, I will help you, I will uphold you with My righteous right hand."

W hen we pray for protection, we pray to be shielded, guarded, defended, and kept in safety. How awesome is this promise that God loves us so much that He will keep us close to Him as we keep Him close to us! You can do anything with God on your side, and you should have no fear knowing that He is a constant source of protection. Second Thessalonians 3:3 (NIV) says "But the Lord is faithful, and he will strengthen you and protect you from the evil one." The promise here is that God will surely preserve us from the effects of the evils that are all around us, and He gives us encouragement through His Word to depend upon His Grace that His protection is sure and certain.

Affirmations:

God, protects me every day, in every way.

I know I am safe, and God continually watches over me.

God walks in front of me and will never lead me on to the wrong path.

Prayer for Tonight:

Father, I come to You, bowing in my heart, asking for protection from the evil one. Lord, I am assailed moment by moment with things of this world that leave me vulnerable to sin of every kind. Surround me with Your divine hedge of protection, and encompass me with Your strength and might. Thank you, Lord.

NIGHT 3–SHIELD AND SHELTER

Psalm 3:3 (NKJV)

"But you, O LORD, are a shield for me, my glory and the One who lifts my head."

The words *shield* and *shelter* are words we associate with warmth, safety, protection, and reassurance. They are good words to describe one facet of our relationship with God, for as His children, we are shielded and sheltered, and kept safe and secure in His protective care. His love and protection surround us. He shelters us when the storms are raging, and shields us when the fires get too hot. Even though we might hang our heads in sorrow, feeling fearful, alone, and vulnerable, if we meditate on His Word, we will soon lift our heads and hands in joy, thanksgiving, and praise.

Affirmations:

My soul waits for the Lord; He is my help and my shield.

I am never alone; my God constantly surrounds me with His presence.

I am secure in the everlasting love of God.

Prayer for Tonight:

Heavenly Father, You cover me with Your hand. Thank you for hiding my soul in the cleft of the rock and sheltering me from my burdens. A blessed Savior You are to me when You give me perfect salvation. Glory to You, God, for being my Redeemer.

NIGHT 4 – SECURITY

Ezekiel 34:25 (KJV)

> "And I will make with them a covenant of peace,
> and will cause the evil beasts to cease out of
> the land: and they shall dwell safely in the wil-
> derness, and sleep in the woods."

This is a direct covenant from God. God is saying that no harm will come to you when you meditate, believe, and act according to His Word. You will always be at peace and will be able to fight off the enemy when attacks come. A mind and heart that has been led even once into this presence knows for all time where to turn to for assistance, reassurance, courage, and guidance. A heart aware of this reservoir of spiritual power within is safe, secure, happy, and peaceful.

Affirmations:

The enemy does not have a hold over me.

I am safe and protected by God in every situation.

I am secure in God's love for me.

Prayer for Tonight:

Heavenly Father, I renew this covenant of peace over my life and the lives of my loved ones. Help me, Lord, so that when the enemy attacks, I know exactly what to say, what to do, and even when to stay silent. Thank you for the security of Your love, peace, and guidance.

NIGHT 5 – PREPARATION

Philippians 4:13 (NKJV)

"I can do all things through Christ who strengthens me."

God will prepare you for every endeavor you embark on. Not only will He prepare you, but He will sustain you through divine love, guidance, wisdom, and strength. If there is a need for healing, make preparation for health. I prepare my mind by keeping watch over my thoughts and words so that they will always be of life. If there is a need for prosperity, make preparation for wealth. I prepare my mind by allowing only thoughts of plenty, success, order, and service to enter it. If there is a need for love, prepare by keeping in tune with God. I realize that I must love to be loved. In all these situations, God will give you the strength needed to carry out these preparations.

Affirmations:

I prepare my life for love by giving love.

I prepare to be healthy, and I am healthy.

I prepare to be prosperous, and I am prosperous.

Prayer for Tonight:

Dear Lord, I begin my prayer in preparation for all that You have for my life. I lay my foundations with a renewed heart through the promises in Your Word. Not only will You prepare me, Lord, but You will sustain me with strength and fortitude for whatever it is that I need. As stone by stone a wall will be laid, so prayer by prayer my preparations will be made.

NIGHT 6–**GUIDANCE**

Psalm 78:14 (NKJV)

"In the daytime also He led them with the cloud, and all the night with a light of fire."

J esus promised that the Spirit of truth would, in His name, come as a teacher, guide, and instructor. From everyday events to major life changes, we have choices to make. However, Jesus did not say *how* the Spirit would help us in making these choices. As we contemplate major life choices, we move from our heads to our hearts. Those who look to the Holy Spirit for guidance find that His instruction is given to all who believe in Christ by direction of that inner voice, or by a dream or vision. When we find peace in that situation or decision, we know that it is the Holy Spirit guiding us to our highest good.

Affirmations:

The voice of God within me is my constant companion and guide.

As I join my heart and mind with the voice of God within me, I am divinely inspired in all that I think, say, and do. The guiding light and love of God fills my life with grace and ease.

Prayer for Tonight:

Loving Father, thank you for being my map of life. As I put my trust in You, I stand on Your truth to lead and guide me on my way to salvation. Just as you parted the Red Sea for Moses and the Israelites, you will safely direct and guide my life in the way it should go.

NIGHT 7–MY STRENGTH

Psalm 46:1 (NKJV)

"God is our refuge and strength, a very present help in trouble."

Worry and fear can keep you awake at night and even consume your dreams. Sometimes we see and hear things that are not really there, and we become anxious and afraid. Know that God will provide safety and will strengthen you through each step of your walk in this life. He will awaken you each morning with a renewed spirit that is ready to face the day ahead.

Affirmations:
My mind is strong, powerful, and calm.
My faith is strong; it helps me stand firm for whatever tomorrow brings.
My body is strong, healthy, and powerful. It is all-renewing, and will be ready for the new day.

Prayer for Tonight:

Dear Father, tonight I ask You to renew my strength. Give me all the power I need to overcome any obstacle, challenge, or troubles in my way. Help me to keep my eyes on You, my Lord. With You there by my side and working through me, I know I can make it. Thank you.

NIGHT 8–HOPE

Isaiah 40:31 (NKJV)

"But those who wait on the LORD shall renew their strength;they shall mount up with wings like eagles, they shall run and not be weary, they shall walk and not faint."

This verse challenges us to know God, proclaim His Word, and wait on Him for strength in our hopes for our future. Things do not always go as we hope, but we can't become impatient or give up through negative thinking and words. Proverbs 18:21 (KJV) says, "Death and life are in the power of the tongue." That's what the enemy wants us to do: choose death. Instead, we choose life by thinking and speaking positive words into our lives and knowing that God's plan is the right plan. Therefore, we have to meditate on God's Word, proclaim it, and wait patiently for His timely outcome. Then our hope will be renewed and outcomes will be manifested through our strength and faith.

Affirmations:

I muster up hope and courage from deep inside me.
I refuse to give up on my dreams and desires.
My God will sustain me in my time of waiting.

Prayer for Tonight:

Heavenly Father, I am your humble servant. I come before You now in need of hope. There are times when I feel helpless. There are times when I feel weak. I pray for hope, and I pray to be filled with Your light during my time of waiting.

NIGHT 9 – **CONFIDENCE**

Job 11:18 (NIV)

"And you will be secure, because there is hope; you will look about you and take your rest in safety."

J eremiah and the people of Judah knew pain and heartache. They had come under the oppression of Babylonia and were torn away from their homeland. Defeat and destruction led to grief and hopelessness. But God gave the prophet some words of hope. He says in Jeremiah 31:3 (NLT), "I have loved you, my people, with an everlasting love. With unfailing love I have drawn you to myself." We remain confident in the everlasting, unchanging love of our Heavenly Father. We have eternal hope that we can go about this earthly life in God's protection.

Affirmations:

God's love for me is everlasting.

There is hope through the love of God.

I am confident that nothing will change God's love for me.

Prayer for Tonight:

Dear God, You know my heart, and You know that I love you, but sometimes I lose focus and start looking to the world to tell me who I am. When my confidence fails me, remind me of the truth that confidence can only be found in chasing after You. Thank you, Father.

NIGHT 10–**WAITING PATIENTLY**

Habakkuk 2:3 (NIV)

"For the revelation awaits an appointed time;
it speaks of the end and will not prove false.
Though it linger, wait for it; it will certainly come
and will not delay."

When the Lord opened Habakkuk's eyes to see the deplorable spiritual and moral condition that existed in Israel in his day, the prophet complained to the Lord concerning the great depths to which the chosen people had fallen. He prayed to the Lord concerning the situation, thinking that the Lord ought to rectify the condition at once. Whenever a person has a longing to know the will of God and asks the Lord to show us light, understanding and answers, God gives it. However, the Lord gives it in His timing, so we must learn to wait patiently.

Affirmations:

My soul is waiting silently because my expectation is from God.

I know that everything comes gradually and at its appointed time.

I easily wait for when the time will be right.

Prayer for Tonight:

Lord, I am seeking Your peace and patience. I want to learn to wait patiently for You to bring answers to my prayers. Help me to cooperate with Your plans for me. As I wait on You, I will continue to turn to Your Word for comfort and direction. Thank you for assuring me that Your plans for me are good and that Your answers will come at the right time.

NIGHT 11 – **STEADFASTNESS**

Mark 9:24 (NKJV)

"Immediately the father of the child cried out and said with tears 'Lord, I believe; help my unbelief.'"

When everything is going smoothly in life, it is easy for us to remember that all things are working together for our good. Then we can affirm that God is in charge of our lives and affairs, and we see all things working perfectly. But when things do not appear to be going well, we have to try harder to remember God's promises and to remain steadfast in our belief. Yes, this is the very time when we need to stand firm and discipline our thoughts so that doubt does not manifest in our minds. By being steadfast in belief at this time and pressing past the place of doubt, we gain rich rewards in our spiritual growth. Because of this spiritual enrichment we can now fulfill the promise of Romans 8:28 (NKJV) "And we know that all things work together for good to those who love God, to those who are the called according to His purpose".

Affirmations:

I press past the place of doubt. I remain steadfast in my faith in God.

My soul is waiting on You, Lord, and I ask You to keep my eyes and my hope on Your love.

I am strong and confident, and my faith and belief carries me to victory.

Prayer for Tonight:

Almighty God, I ask You to grant me divine grace to live in faith. Take away all doubt, fear, and unbelief from my heart. Even when circumstances do not line up with what I want, give me wisdom to know that everything happens by divine order.

In Jesus name, amen.

NIGHT 12–OUR BEST FRIEND

Deuteronomy 31:6 (NKJV)

> "Be strong and of good courage, do not fear nor
> be afraid of them; for the LORD your God, He is
> the One that goes with you. He will never leave
> you nor forsake you."

What a privilege and blessing to have Jesus as our friend;He is a friend who will never leave us or forsake us. He intercedes for us before the Father and supplies all our needs. He forgives all our sins, understands our sorrows, gives us new mercies every day, and provides us sufficient grace in times of trouble. He is indeed our best friend.

Affirmations:

I am a friend of God; He calls me friend.
He will never leave me or forsake me.
His grace is sufficient for me.

Prayer for Tonight:

Heavenly Father, You are my best friend and a price-less gift to me. You hear my every prayer, know my every desire and You give comfort whenever needed. I bless our friendship, Lord. Thank you that I am forever in Your heart, as You are in mine.

NIGHT 13–OUR LOVING COUNSELOR

Psalm 16:7 (NKJV)

"I will bless the LORD who has given me counsel;
my heart also instructs me in the night seasons."

Could you imagine receiving a check for $100 million and never using it as a resource to help someone, or even help yourself? What a shame that would be if you wasted such an opportunity. So, what must God our Father think of what we have not done with the precious gift of His Holy Spirit? Jesus asked our Father to give us a counselor who would instruct us and lead us into all truth. When we become children of God, we receive His Holy Spirit into our lives, yet we barely know how to access this third part of the Trinity. We have been given spiritual gifts, but we don't know what they are or how they work. God has indwelled us with the person of the Holy Spirit to instruct us, guide us, and teach us how to access all that He has for us.

Affirmations:

Holy Spirit, I give You my heart and offer my thanks for Your graceful teachings.

Grant me the gift of knowledge, that I might understand Your counsel.

As I follow Your guidance, I walk without deviation into the path of eternal salvation.

Prayer for Tonight:

Dear God, thank you for giving me the gift of the Holy Spirit and making me conscious of this presence in my life. Teach me, O Lord, to activate the spiritual gifts that You have bestowed upon me. In Jesus name, amen.

NIGHT 14–**INTIMACY**

Jeremiah 33:3 (NKJV)

"Call to Me, and I will answer you, and show you great and mighty things, which you do not know."

God doesn't want our interactions with Him to end at salvation. If we communicate with Him only on a surface level, we cheat ourselves and hinder fulfillment of His ultimate goal for us: an intimate relationship with Him. Though this is His desire for each of His children, many believers do not live in the close fellowship He's made available to them. So how can we achieve intimacy with God? We welcome God into our lives wholeheartedly, and we accept Jesus Christ as His Son and our Savior. We meditate on His Word, and we follow His guidance. We constantly seek Him, and when we find Him, we stay close through faith and fellowship.

Affirmations:

I will make God my priority and put Him first in my life.

I will obey God's commandments.

I will pray to my Heavenly Father without ceasing.

Prayer for Tonight:

Heavenly Father, I make you a priority in my life. I seek you wholeheartedly Lord, out of desperation, out of desire and also out of discipline, because I know my life is dependent on Your grace. Help me to pray continually, so that my relationship with You remains intimate and strong. Thank you.

NIGHT 15 – **LIVING WATER**

Lamentations 2:19 (NKJV)

"Arise, cry out in the night, at the beginning of the watches; pour out your heart like water before the face of the Lord. Lift your hands toward Him for the life of your children, who faint from hunger at the head of every street."

Your burdens will be released if you pour your heart out to God. Write down everything that's on your mind, and pray about it. At times, the burdens can seem too heavy, but they will become lighter after pouring your heart out and praising God for the victory. Deuteronomy 4:30 promises us that "when you are in distress and all these things have happened to you, then in later days you will return to the Lord your God and obey him" (NIV). If we listen and take heed ofHis promises, His mercies will rain down on us, and our thirsts will always be quenched.

Affirmations:

My burdens are light and not heavy.

I will pour out my heart to the Lord.

I will drink from the fountain of the living water and be satisfied.

Prayer for Tonight:

My soul is thirsty for You, Lord. Look into my heart and fill the emptiness that only You can reach. I lift my cup to You and ask You to overflow it with Your Word. Thank you for raining Your mercies down on me. I remember Your promise, O Lord, that says, "I am the bread of life. He who comes to Me shall never hunger, and he who believes in Me shall never thirst" (John 6:35, NKJV).

NIGHT 16–**REFRESHING**

Proverbs 3:24 (NKJV)

"When you lie down, you will not be afraid; yes, you will lie down and your sleep will be sweet."

As believers, we experience a time of refreshing by quieting our hearts in a devotional time of prayer. When we spend time alone with the Lord, we can experience His peace and joy, which renews and refreshes us in spirit. There is another kind of refreshing that we can expect from God. It is physical refreshing. God says that at the end of the day, you should look forward to sleep and rest, and enjoy His presence in the night hours. He will keep you safe, and will renew and refresh your body and mind to face the new day ahead.

Affirmations:

My thoughts are filled with faith rather than fear.

My spiritual life is renewed and refreshed through the Word of God.

My body is a holy temple filled with divine, renewing life.

Prayer for Tonight:

Precious Lord, as You help me to share my heart with You in prayer, my spirit is refreshed. As I lay down to sleep, I let peace and relaxation wash over me. Thank you, Father, that as I draw near to You, my mind and body are refreshed and renewed.

NIGHT 17–**PROVISION**

1 Kings 19:5–6 (NKJV)

> "Then as he lay and slept under a broom tree, suddenly an angel touched him, and said to him, 'Arise and eat.' Then he looked, and there by his head was a cake baked on coals, and a jar of water. So he ate and drank, and lay down again."

E lijah lay down and slept under a broom tree, but he was awakened out of his sleep and found himself not only well provided for with bread and water, but also attended to by an angel, who guarded him when he slept. God loves us so much that he continuously provides us with all that we need. We don't have to worry about lacking what we need. Everything is there for us. Matthew 6:25–27 (NKJV) comes to mind:"Therefore I say to you, do not worry about your life, what you will eat or what you will drink; nor about your body, what you will put on. Is not life more than food and the body more than clothing? Look at the birds of the air, for they neither sow nor reap nor gather into barns; yet your heavenly Father feeds them. Are you not of more value than they? Which of you by worrying can add one cubit to his stature?"

Affirmations:

My God will supply all of my needs.

Abundance is within me and around me, and comes through me.

There is no lack in my life; my harvest is here.

Prayer for Tonight:

Divine Father, my heart yearns to express my love for You. Thank you for Your grace. Thank you for knowing exactly what I need before I even ask. Thank you for never abandoning me or leaving me begging for bread. Thank you for being my faithful source.

NIGHT 18 – LEAVING IT ALL IN HIS HANDS

Ruth 3:4 (NKJV)

> "Then it shall be, when he lies down, that you
> shall notice the place where he lies; and you
> shall go in, uncover his feet, and lie down; and
> he will tell you what you should do."

R uth had to cast herself at Boaz's feet. She didn't know what would happen next or what his reaction would be, but she knew that she needed to be where he was, and that meant the threshing floor. Have you ever felt like that? You're going through a time of testing and there's nowhere to turn to for help. All you can do is throw yourself down at the Lord's feet, not really knowing what will happen next. To us, this seems like a huge risk, but to God, it is the very place He wants us to be, totally dependent on Him as we leave everything up to Him. There is a quote that says, "Those who leave everything in God's hand will eventually see God's hand in everything." Yes, let us not forfeit the blessing of God by taking things into our own hands. Instead, let us enter into His trust, live in His peace and receive His joy.

Affirmations:
I am divinely guided in the direction I should go.
I hold onto God's hand, and I'm never letting go.
I come to the throne of grace for my life, and remain there.

Prayer for Tonight:
Dear Lord, thank you for allowing me to come to Your throne to rest and wait. Help me to know that when I give my burdens to You, I'm never to take them back. You will guide and instruct me in the way that I should go to reach the place where I need to be.

NIGHT 19 – PRAISING HIM IN EVERYTHING

Psalm 149:5 (ESV)

"Let the godly exult in glory; let them sing for joy on their beds."

L et us praise God, from whom all blessings flow. Praising God and giving thanks to Him for every blessing, no matter how small it may seem, is one of the quickest ways of realizing the fulfillment of our desires. It is the surest way of opening the channel for the inflow of God's life, joy, and love. Let us praise God for the victory that He has commanded for our lives. Continuously praise Him for turning our situations around favorably and for the answered prayers that He has granted.

Affirmations:

I sing praises to the Lord, for He is good to me.

I give thanks and praise to the Lord Almighty, for His love endures forever.

Heavenly Father, thank you for filling my heart with thanksgiving.

Prayer for Tonight:

Abba Father, I praise You because You are trustworthy and true. You are my teacher, and Your understanding and wisdom is beyond anything that I can imagine. You have commanded victory over my life, and I am eternally grateful. You are the way, the truth, and the life, Lord. I love that You delight in me and rejoice over me with singing. I will forever praise Your holy name, O Lord.

NIGHT 20 – JOY

Psalm 30:5 (NKJV)

"For His anger is but for a moment, His favor is for life; weeping may endure for a night, but joy comes in the morning."

God shows us that He can become angry with us, but only for a brief moment. We know this when we become convicted about something, when we know without a shadow of doubt that we need to repent for something that we have done. But because God is love, His anger only lasts a moment. His favor, however, will last for a lifetime. Thus, if we repent of our sins and seek and obey His counsel, we will ultimately live a life full of favor and joy.

Affirmations:

I project joy to everyone with whom I interact.

I joyfully honor the flow of life, and I allow it to wash over me and to deliver me to blissful places.

Joy is abundant within my soul, and it bursts into my life in unexpected ways.

Prayer for Tonight:

Precious Father, You have me in the palm of your hand. Even though I may be in a dark place, You strengthen me and bring me through it triumphantly. Thank you for being my joy and salvation.

NIGHT 21 – MAKING TIME FOR GOD

Luke 6:12 (NASB)

"It was at this time that He went off to the mountain to pray, and He spent the whole night in prayer to God."

Deep down, we desperately desire to connect with God—and He wants to connect with you. However, figuring out how to do that can seem difficult. After all, God is God. He's huge and mysterious and greater than us. He's everywhere, yet He's invisible. So we don't connect with God in the same way we would with a friend. Yet He asks us to come and spend time with Him. So how do we connect with the invisible God? The answer is simple. We make it a habit. We set aside specific time to spend time with Him by talking to Him and listening for His answers.

Affirmations:

I will spend more time in the presence of God.

I will keep my connection to God through prayer and devotion.

My answers come from God. I will listen for them.

Prayer for Tonight:

Precious Lord, thank you for hearing my every prayer. Help me to commit to establishing a direct connection to You by spending time in Your presence. Give me wisdom and discernment to know Your answers when I ask, seek, and knock.

NIGHT 22–**WORKING FOR JESUS**

Revelation 7:15 (NASB)

"For this reason, they are before the throne of God; and they serve Him day and night in His temple; and He who sits on the throne will spread His tabernacle over them."

B eing of service requires commitment and effort, and sometimes the rewards are huge. I can be of service at work as I assist my coworkers on projects. I can be of service in my community as I volunteer for special events. I can be of service with family as I help with daily tasks. I can also be of service to organizations that are meaningful to me, or that need my assistance and expertise. As such, I choose to thrive, excel, and work diligently with a sincere heart for my heavenly Father.

Affirmations:

As I work for Jesus, I set the law of giving and receiving into motion.

The one thing I can do that will never fail is God's work, and being His servant to others.

My acts of helpful activity bless me as I am blessing others.

Prayer for Tonight:

Precious Father, the fields are full, but the workers are few. You have called me to service, and I ask that You send Your spirit to make me strong in faith and active in service to others. God of love, keep me close and help me to serve with a humble heart.

NIGHT 23 – THE LIGHT OF LIFE

John 12:46 (NKJV)

> "I have come as a light into the world, that whoever believes in Me should not abide in darkness."

Just as the darkness of the night turns into the light of the day, our innermost fears and anxieties—and the darkness we may feel because of them—will soon dissipate if we believe. As we focus on God, He will lighten our path to redemption, safety, and peace. We must speak words of faith. We must align our thoughts with positivity rather than negativity. We must "let go and let God."

Affirmations:

I am centered in God, and I maintain a clear vision.

I make a positive difference; I speak only faith-filled words.

God is the fulfillment of all my needs.

Prayer for Tonight:

Dear God, I believe that You are the Light of the World. Thank you for leading me out of the darkness and into the light through Your Word. Help my life to stay bright and positive. Even if the dark clouds come, I know that with You in my heart, and through Your Word, I will overcome them.

NIGHT 24–**OBEDIENCE**

Joshua 1:8 (NKJV)

"This Book of the Law shall not depart from your mouth but you shall meditate in it day and night, that you may observe to do according to all that is written in it. For then you will make your way prosperous, and then you will have good success."

As I obey God's Word, I become one with Him and my path of life is made clear to me. However, obeying God is not a task, but a duty that takes on new meaning for my life. I see that I am obedient to God as I let myself be filled with divine ideas, truth, love, and faith. I am obedient to God as I let Him fill my mind and heart with words and actions that inspire, heal, and encourage.

Affirmations:

Because I know Jesus, I remain in His love.

I live by faith, not by sight.

I follow Jesus, no matter where He leads me.

Prayer for Tonight:

Heavenly Father, I surrender to You all that I am and pray that I may walk in love and stay as humble as Your Son, Jesus Christ, all the days of my life. Help me to take every thought captive and to surrender my heart to You in true obedience. In Jesus name, I pray.

NIGHT 25 – **BLAMELESS BEFORE GOD**

1 Corinthians 1:8 (NIV)

"He will also keep you firm to the end, so that you will be blameless on the day of our Lord Jesus Christ."

Discovering the Spirit of Christ at the heart of our being, we find that our nature is holy and divine, blameless and perfect. However, we are inclined to think often of our faults and imperfections, to look to the side of us that is far from godlike. We need to turn away from those convictions to look for the good in our nature, which was given to us through His death and resurrection. When we do this, we can come before the throne with godlike perfection, knowing that we have been washed clean of our sins and are now blameless before God.

Affirmations:

I am a branch of the true vine, and a conduit of Christ's life.

My old self was crucified with Christ, and I am no longer a slave to sin.

I have been given the righteousness of God in Christ.

Prayer for Tonight:

Holy Lord, I ask you for wisdom, knowledge, and understanding so that I can walk only on the straight and righteous path. Help me not to be blinded to Your truth, so that I can live a blameless and holy life. In Jesus name, amen.

NIGHT 26 – **STAYING FOCUSED**

Psalm 63:6 (NKJV)

"When I remember You on my bed, I meditate on You in the night watches."

God wants you to always keep Him at the forefront of your mind—day and night. Stay focused on Him and His Word. Remember that you are one with God's goodness. Through this awareness, you will attract that which brings happiness and enrichment to your life. Focus your attention on God, who is the true source of all goodness. Do not let the enemy steer you away from your focus. James 4:7 says, "Submit yourselves, then, to God. Resist the devil, and he will flee from you" (NIV).

Affirmations:

I am alert and attentive at all times to God's Word.

I focus my prayer life on seeking God.

My goodness comes from God, which brings enrichment to my life.

Prayer for Tonight:

Heavenly Father, provide me with determination and calmness in my soul. Guard my mind and my thoughts as I pray, so that the enemy will not enter in and destroy with worry and fear. Help me to keep the eyes of my heart focused on You, O Lord, and my ears open to Your leading guidance. In Jesus name, amen.

NIGHT 27 – **FORGIVENESS**

Romans 4:7 (NLT)

"Oh, what joy for those whose disobedience is forgiven, whose sins are put out of sight."

"Forgive us our sins, as we forgive those who have sinned against us." This is part of the Lord's Prayer, which He instructed us to pray. Here, He advocated both goodwill toward others and a principle for furthering our own forgiveness and well-being. To make the best use of present opportunities, we cannot afford to carry either the burden of holding others under condemnation or the regret of our own past mistakes. As we forgive others, we cleanse our minds and hearts of resentment and ill will so that God's love may bring us the forgiveness that we need for ourselves.

Affirmations:

I am capable of moving beyond my mistakes.

I release the past, so I can freely step into the future.

I forgive others as I forgive myself, with ease, sincerity, and loving compassion.

Prayer for Tonight:

Dear Lord, I know I am a sinner, and I ask for Your forgiveness for my transgressions, whether they be intentional or unintentional. I believe You died for my sins and rose from the dead. I trust and follow You as my Lord and Savior. Guide my life and help me to do Your will. Thank you, Father.

NIGHT 28–**MIGHTY LOVE**

Zephaniah 3:17 (NKJV)

"The LORD your God is in your midst, the Mighty One, will save; He will rejoice over you with gladness, He will quiet you with His love, He will rejoice over you with singing."

This verse should bring so much joy to us. He is God of our salvation, mighty in His love for us. Whatever it is that we need, He will give it. God will do the same for us as we do for Him. He will rejoice with us, He will be our quiet when we need peace away from the raging storms, and He will exult over us when we overcome through him. Deuteronomy 30:9 (NKJV) says, "The LORD your God will make you abound in all the work of your hand, in the fruit of your body, in the increase of your livestock, and in the produce of your land for good. For the LORD will again rejoice over you for good as He rejoiced over your fathers."

Affirmations:

God is love, and I open my heart to receive Him.
God will supply all my needs, whatever they are.
I will praise God at all times, for His love endures forever.

Prayer for Tonight:

Holy One, You are the source of all life, all grace, and all blessings. Thank you for the gift of life that enables me to be me. Thank you for the breath of life that guides my heartbeat each and every day. Thank you for the food of this earth that nurtures my life. Thank you for the quiet time when I need it, and thank you for the rejoicing that You give me in answered prayer.

NIGHT 29 – **LIMITLESS**

Psalm 42:8 (NKJV)

"The LORD will command His loving kindness in the daytime, and in the night His song shall me with me—a prayer to the God of my life."

As parents, we love our children unconditionally. We would do anything to make them feel loved, cared for, and protected. As God's child, there is no limit to how much He loves us. He is faithful to us no matter what, and He is always waiting with open arms to receive us, love us, direct us, and forgive us.

Affirmations:

Through God's direction, I am one with limitless life and love.

As I open myself to God, I am filled with inspiration and new opportunities.

My loved ones are filled with the joy of living. They are triumphant and victorious in every situation.

Prayer for Tonight:

Thank you, God, for Your unending love. Thank you for being faithful to me even when I am not faithful to You. Thank you for receiving my prayers and for blessing me in every area of my life.

NIGHT 30 – **MY PEACE I GIVE TO YOU**

Psalm 4:8 (NKJV)

"I will both lie down in peace, and sleep; for You alone, O LORD, make me dwell in safety."

God will keep you safe during the night, and will grant you peaceful dreams. Speak your worries out loud to God, and use His power to overcome whatever is making you feel unsafe. As you keep your mind on your Heavenly Father, sleep in His perfect peace and safety. You will become so established in the peace of God that there is no room in your mind, heart, or life to feel anything but safe.

Affirmations:

I can overcome anything by the power of God.

Nothing can disturb the calm peace of my soul.

I will rest in the harmonious and serene peace of God.

Prayer for Tonight:

Almighty God, give me peace in my mind, body, soul, and spirit. Heal and remove everything that is causing any stress, grief, or sorrow. Guide my path and let Your peace continue to reign in everything I lay my hands on. Let Your angels of peace go ahead of me when I go out, have them stay by my side when I return, and let them surround me as I take my rest. In Jesus name, amen.

NIGHT 31 – BE COMFORTED

Matthew 6:34 (NKJV)

"Therefore do not worry about tomorrow, for tomorrow will worry about its own things. Sufficient for the day is its own trouble."

Maybe you have an unpleasant meeting in the morning, or are awaiting results from the doctor. Are the battles with your children becoming overwhelming? Are unpaid bills piling up? When the heart is full of anxiety, there is one sure way to ease this feeling and rise above it. You are comforted by the Spirit of truth within you. You are strengthened by His presence, which is always with you. God wants to change your fear, worry, and anxiety into comfort and the assurance that you are never alone.

Affirmations:

My life is full of peace; I am not anxious about my future.
My steps are directed by faith rather than fear.
I am a child of God; He will never leave me or forsake me.

Prayer for Tonight:

Heavenly Father, even though my heart is heavy sometimes, I want to praise Your name. You are an awesome God. You spoke and the world was created. With You, nothing is impossible. Take away all fear and anxiety from me, O Lord. I give You all the glory and honor for who You are and what You do for me. Amen.

Lesley A is a mother, grandmother and friend. She has been in a relationship with God for over ten years and knows that Jesus Christ is her Lord and Savior. Lesley A believes that if we put God first in everything, we will live the best life that He created us to live.

GOD BLESS YOU ALL